GOLD FEVER
Finding a Fortune

Robyn P. Watts

KNOWLEDGE
BOOKS AND SOFTWARE

5

Teacher Notes:

Gold can form the topic for extended discussions and investigations in earth sciences. Gold and making a fortune is always a good story and this leads to many associated investigations of the history of settlement of Australia and the wealth that was created.

Discussion activities for consideration:

1. Where was the gold found in Victoria? Is gold still mined in Victoria?

2. Why is gold important? How much would an ounce of gold cost today?

3. How did the miners get the gold? How do big mining companies get gold today?

4. What did the discovery of gold do for Australia? Discuss issues like immigration, population growth, infrastructure, mining, and tourism.

Difficult words to be introduced and practised before reading this book: chemical, jewellery, pendants, bangles, earrings, bracelets, electronic, equipment, notebooks, screens, medical, conditions, rheumatoid, arthritis, dentists, sometimes, decorate, vehicles, radiation, plastics, different, bendable, oxidise, companies, Moliagul, weird, quartz, searching, crystal, volcanic, sedimentary, metamorphic, alluvial.

Acknowledgement of the First Nations' People: We acknowledge the Traditional Owners of country throughout Australia and recognise their continuing connection to land, waters and culture. We pay our respects to their Elders past, present and emerging. kilometres, rescue, information, understanding.

Contents

1. Getting the Gold

Gold is worth a lot of money which is why everyone is after it. Gold has been used for a long time to hold riches.

The chemical symbol for gold is Au. Gold is used to make jewellery. Can you think of types of jewellery that contain gold?

Gold can be found in rings, chains, pendants, bangles, earrings, and bracelets.

There are many other uses for gold. Small amounts of gold can be found in computers and other electronic equipment such as mobile phones, notebooks and screens.

Small amounts of gold are used in medicines to treat medical conditions such as rheumatoid arthritis. Dentists sometimes use gold to fill teeth.

Gold is used to decorate and protect other metals. One example of this is gold-plated bathroom taps.

2. Gold Has Many Uses.

Besides computers and tech stuff, gold is also used in space vehicles.

The lunar lander was covered in gold foil. The gold stops radiation and heating. The gold is also used on moving parts in space. It does not wear like other materials.

Other materials like plastics will break up from the Sun's radiation. The gold foil does not get damaged by radiation.

Why is gold used in so many different ways? Gold or Au is a stable element. It doesn't corrode or rust. It is malleable, which means it is bendable when soft and pure. Gold does not rust like steel.

Gold can be mixed with other metals to make strong objects that still look like gold. This can be used for jewellery, cups, medals, and other items. These are stronger and do not bend like pure gold.

At the Olympics you see many winners biting the gold medal. This is to prove it is gold as pure gold is softer than mixed metals.

Gold is a metal that people trade. Many people and big companies mine for gold.

What did the early miners do with the gold they found? The gold miners sold the gold and received money for their find.

What would you do if you found gold?

Would you sell it?

Some people find gold and make their gold into jewellery and wear it.

What would you choose to do?

Have they mined all the gold on the Earth's surface? No! There are many big companies mining for gold in Australia and around the world.

Many men, women, and children go mining for gold, hoping to find treasure.

What did the early miners do with the gold they found?

The gold miners sold the gold and received money for their find. Some became really rich - that is why they got gold fever.

3. Where Was the Biggest Gold Nugget Found?

The biggest gold nugget in the world was found in 1869 in Bulldog Creek at Moliagul, in Victoria, Australia.

The gold nugget weighed 78 kilograms. It was found by John Deason and Richard Oates and they named the nugget "Welcome Stranger".

What would you name a nugget of gold?

A kilo of gold today is worth $81,300.00 Australian dollars. And they found 78 kilograms! About $6.3 million today!

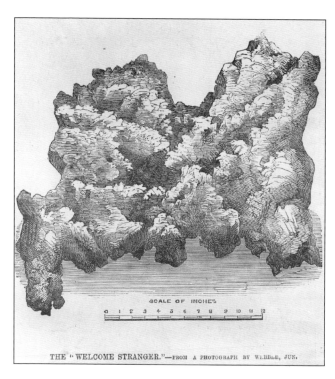

SCALE OF INCHES

0 1 2 3 4 5 6 7 8 9 10 11 12

THE " WELCOME STRANGER."—FROM A PHOTOGRAPH BY WEBBER, JUN.

Where was the world-famous gold nugget found? Was it found in cliffs or along a sandy river?

Where do you find gold?

Gold is sometimes found in streams. And sometimes gold is found in mountain cliffs.

This giant gold nugget was found in the sandy soil of a dried-out river gully around the root of a tree. A very weird place for a giant piece of gold.

How did they find "Welcome Stranger"?

In 1869 John Deason, a miner from Cornwall, England, had been mining with his mate, Richard Oates, for seven years. While searching near some tree roots, Deason discovered just below the surface, a gold nugget. It must have just been sticking out and there were large bits of quartz around it. Deason broke a pick handle trying to lever it out of the ground and eventually extracted it with a crowbar. Deason, with his partner Richard Oates, hid the nugget until dark. Then, with Oates, he dug it out and took it home in a horse and cart. The bank bought it and turned it into gold bars.

The "Welcome Stranger" was found in 1869 at Moliagul in Victoria. Moliagul is located at one corner of a district known as the Golden Triangle. This area has produced more gold nuggets than anywhere in Australia. Victoria is the world's home of giant gold nuggets.

The other towns that form the triangle are Tarnagulla and Dunolly. Although there are few houses, most of which are in ruins, there are about 200 people still living in the district. This area used to be a busy gold mining town, but now it is a very quiet old ghost town. To see what these gold mining towns were like during those times, you can visit Bendigo to get a sense of the size of the gold rush.

4. Where Do You Find Gold?

What type of rock is gold found in? Gold can be found in quartz rocks.

What does quartz look like? Quartz is commonly found as a clear crystal rock. It looks like glass but has a crystal structure. Quartz can also have a grey colour due to the presence of tin. Quartz can also be a pink colour and this type of quartz is called rose quartz. Where there are gold-bearing areas and there are quartz rocks, it is possible that gold can be found.

Quartz is commonly a clear crystal rock, usually found running as seams.

23

There are three types of rocks in the Earth's crust.

There are the volcanic rocks which come from the volcanoes. Examples of volcanic rocks are basalt and granite.

The second type of rock is sedimentary rock. The sedimentary rocks are made up of cemented sediments being pushed together over time. Examples of sedimentary rocks are sandstone made of sand particles.

The third type of rock is metamorphic rock. Metamorphic rocks form when heat and pressure are applied to the rock and the rock is changed.

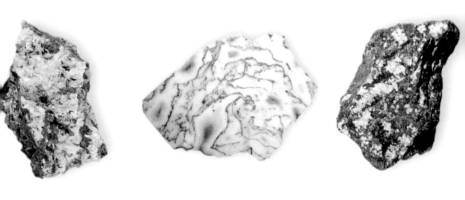

25

Where do you think quartz will mostly be found? Remember gold and quartz are found together. Look for quartz to find gold!

Will quartz be found in sedimentary rock? No!

Will quartz be found in volcanic rock? Yes! Most of the quartz has been found with volcanic rock.

Quartz is the hardest common mineral. The hardest mineral in the world is diamond, however quartz is the hardest common mineral on the Earth's surface.

Most of the gold has been found with volcanic rock. Volcanic rock can be broken down and washed and tumbled in a creek. The rock is broken down by wind, water and other rocks tumbling against each other. Little particles of gold and quartz can tumble out of the rock into deposits near streams. This type of gold is called alluvial gold.

This is where the gold miners looked for gold. In the streams, they panned for gold.

How do you mine for alluvial gold? You will need a gold pan and a shovel. A gold pan is a dish. Choose an area where you think you might find gold.

Look for an area that has quartz pieces in the soil near a creek. Use the shovel to scoop a few handfuls of gravel, sand and silt out of the creek into your pan. You then wash the dirt with water. The water will wash the soil and you may spot the fleck of quartz minerals. At the very bottom of the gold pan, you might find gold flecks. The gold settles at the bottom of the pan because it is heavy. Look closely for the gold flecks.

Gold particles are found in streams, creeks and river soil where the water is fast then slows down. When the water slows down, it drops the gold flecks.

Why does the water drop the gold flecks?

The water drops the gold and quartz particles because there is not enough energy in the water to carry the gold flecks. When the water is moving fast, it can carry the heavy pieces, but when the water slows down, it drops them.

Gold flecks can be found where the water has run fast and then slowed down.

Gold is heavier than other things in the river, so roughly shake and swirl the pan around to help the gold settle at the bottom of the pan. Hopefully, you will see the gold flecks at the bottom of the pan.

People also use sluicing trays to roll the water around in trays. Gold miners pick out the flecks of gold from the sluicing trays. People still go looking for gold and some make a fortune.

Today there are many huge gold mining companies. These still use the sluicing tray but on a huge scale. Most of the mines today are big businesses. They need to get big trucks and crushers to get enough gold.

5. Can You Still Find Gold?

All metal detectors will find gold nuggets if they're in the ground, and if they are big enough. Swimmers can lose their jewellery on the beach. Metal detectors can find lost gold jewellery in the sand on a beach. Metal detectors can find coins. Metal detectors have found gold.

Recently, an Australian man unearthed a 1.4kg gold nugget with a metal detector while wandering Western Australia's gold fields.

A shop in Kalgoorlie shared pictures of the rock online, estimated to be worth $100,000.

6. What is Gold Fever?

Gold Fever occurs when gold is found and many people rush to the area to find gold. There is a town called Hill End, near Bathurst, where a gold rush occurred. This occurred in 1885 when gold was discovered.

A Hill End miner had been mining for years without finding anything. His name was Bernhardt Otto Holtermann and in1885, he found gold at Hill End. Hill End is now a township with a population of 102 people, according to the census in 2016.

Weight : 630 lbs
Height : 4ft 9in
Width : 2ft 3in
Average Thickness 4 inches
Value £1500..

In 1885, Hill End was known as Bald
Hill. The settlement would have been
a tent town. At the height of the gold
rush era, there was a population of
about 8,000 people living in Hill End.
The Royal Hotel is the sole remaining
hotel from the 52 that used to operate
in the town. Parts of the old gold town
now look like a ghost town. Looking at
the town, you can see signs of old
brick buildings that look like a bakery,
an old bank, a pub and even still see
old mine shafts.

Different people flocked to Hill End in the hope of finding the same type of treasure Bernhardt had found.

What did he find?

Remember, he had been mining for years without any success. He found a quartz rock and embedded inside it was a gold nugget.

The gold nugget was 59 centimetres long, weighing 290 kg. It had an estimated gold content of 93 kg. It made him very rich. He built a mansion in North Sydney called "The Towers". It had a stained-glass window showing him and the nugget.

There was a gold fossicker who kept a mining map in a suitcase. This mine map had definite places located on the map where he thought he could find gold. The locked suitcase was left with a friend for safe-keeping. The gold fossicker visited the town to make a claim on the land for miner's rights. Something happened to the fossicker, and no one knows why he did not return to collect his suitcase.

The friend did not open the suitcase. The suitcase never got opened for years. Would you open the suitcase? After years of waiting for the gold miner to collect his suitcase, it still remains locked waiting for the gold miner's return.

Word Bank

chemical	dentists	crystal
jewellery	sometimes	volcanic
pendants	decorate	sedimentary
bangles	vehicles	metamorphic
earrings	radiation	alluvial
bracelets	plastics	
electronic	different	
equipment	bendable	
notebooks	oxidise	
screens	companies	
medical	Moliagul	
conditions	weird	
rheumatoid	quartz	
arthritis	searching	